Once a Week Comprehension

Haydn Perry

Book 2

Ginn is an imprint of Pearson Education Limited, a company incorporated in England and Wales, having its registered office at Edinburgh Gate, Harlow, Essex, CM20 2JE. Registered company number: 872828

www.ginn.co.uk

Text © Haydn Perry, 1960

This revised edition 2008

20 19 18 17 16 15 14 13
IMP: 16 15 14 13 12 11 10

British Library Cataloguing in Publication Data is available from the British Library on request.

ISBN 978 0 435996 73 4

Typeset by Planman Technologies India Pvt. Ltd
Cover design by Tony Richardson
Cover photo © iStockPhoto.com
Printed by Multivista Global Ltd

Every effort has been made to contact copyright holders of material reproduced in this book. Any omissions will be rectified in subsequent printings if notice is given to the publishers.

PREFACE

This book of thirty comprehension pieces is intended to develop the intensive reading ability of children in their middle Primary School years. The passages are graded in difficulty. They are followed by questions that test the student's understanding of the text, and by a wide range of language exercises aimed at improving grammar and composition skills, and increasing the student's vocabulary.

TO THE PUPIL

In each of the thirty tests there are five questions.

Read each question carefully, so that you understand exactly what you are asked to do before you begin.

Do not spend too long on any one question. You should answer all five questions in 45 minutes.

Make sure that you have not missed a question, or part of one.

If you find that you have made a mistake, alter your work clearly and neatly so that your teacher will know what it is you mean him or her to read and mark.

HAYDN PERRY

A NOTE FROM THE PUBLISHERS

In this new edition, each of the exercises has been given a heading to help students identify the topics they are working on. Some of the passages and exercises have also been edited to ensure that the content and usage of language are up to date.

TEST 1

(A) Read through the following passage very carefully, and then answer the questions.

The Battle of Hastings

The Battle of Hastings was fought in 1066 in the south of England. The English, who were led by Harold, had taken up the best position at the top of the Senlac Hill. The Norman soldiers tried repeatedly to dislodge them, but the English had driven wooden stakes into the ground and formed their shields into a wall. From the shelter of these, they were able to force their enemies back down the hill time and time again.

William the Norman, whom we now call William the Conqueror, decided he would try to win the battle by other means. His archers had been unable to reach the English soldiers because the shield wall was able to block the arrows. He ordered his archers to shoot their arrows high into the air so that they would fall on to the heads of the English. In time, many defenders were killed in this way.

The greatest disaster came when an arrow pierced the eye of the English king himself. Harold fell to the ground and his soldiers, seeing their leader slain, fled from the hill in confusion. So died Harold, The Last of the English Kings.

1 Who were the two leaders in this battle?
2 What other names are given to these two leaders?
3 Where did the battle take place: (*a*) on the banks of a river; (*b*) on the slopes of a hill; (*c*) around the walls of a castle?
4 Why was it difficult for the Normans to drive out the English?
5 What plan did the Normans use in an effort to gain the victory?
6 Why had the shooting of arrows in the usual way proved to be a failure?
7 What was 'the greatest disaster'?
8 What words or phrases in the story mean: (*a*) drive them out; (*b*) stuck into; (*c*) in fear and disorder?

9   Why did the English finally run away?
10   Were the defenders: (*a*) the Normans, led by William; (*b*) the people who were looking on; (*c*) the English, led by Harold?

B   Similes

When we wish to say that something is **red**, we may say it is **as red as blood**.

Choose the correct answers from these:

1   As black as: (*a*) a mole; (*b*) a hole; (*c*) coal.
2   As brown as: (*a*) a lorry; (*b*) a berry; (*c*) a beret.
3   As green as: (*a*) grass; (*b*) paint; (*c*) a carpet.
4   As blue as: (*a*) a butterfly; (*b*) the sky; (*c*) a gate.

C   Compound words

Here are two words: **grape** and **vine**. From these we can make the word **grapevine**.

Make four new compound words from the following:

finger	tea	lace	arm
shoe	fire	print	spoon

D   Collective nouns

A number of **chicks** together is called a **brood**. What words could be used for:

1   A _______ of fish
2   A _______ of bees
3   A _______ of buffaloes
4   A _______ of birds

E   More than one

Rewrite these sentences so that they mean more than one.

Example: *The **tree** grew tall. The **trees** grew tall.*

1   The day and night seemed long.
2   The berry lay near the leaf.
3   The bird sat on the chimney.
4   The monkey bit the lady.
5   The watch lay in the gutter.

TEST 2

(A) Read through the following passage very carefully, and then answer the questions.

Theras

Theras was seven years old, and because he was seven he was to go to school. That was the custom of the city in which he lived. It was an exciting day for everyone in the house, most of all for Theras. Until this time he had had to stay at home with his mother and the servants, and was allowed to play only in the house, or in the street close by the front door. Now he was to go out to school with the other boys. Now he would often be with his father, going to and fro in the city. He already felt grown up.

Now to start. Theras's mother put on him his long, outdoor cloak; for in the house he wore only one garment, like a shirt, reaching to his knees. His mother kissed him. You might have thought he was going miles away.

C. D. Snedeker

1 What important thing was happening to Theras?
2 Why was this to happen?
3 With whom had he always been until this time?
4 Where had he been allowed to play?
5 What garment would he wear out of doors?
6 Why might you have thought he was going miles away:
   (*a*) because of his outdoor clothes; (*b*) because of the fuss his mother made of him; (*c*) because he really was going miles away?
7 Why did he feel 'grown up': (*a*) because he had suddenly grown tall; (*b*) because his father carried him on his shoulders; (*c*) because he was going to and fro in the city?
8 Write down the sentences that are true: (*a*) Theras lived in a small village. (*b*) He was seven years old. (*c*) He lived in a city. (*d*) He was nine years old. (*e*) His parents were wealthy. (*f*) He came from a poor family.

Ⓑ Spot the mistakes

There are mistakes in each of these sentences. Write the sentences correctly.

1   He is taller than me.
2   Could you see who done it?
3   He sang that song very nice.
4   The teacher rung the bell at twelve o'clock.
5   The match had just began.

Ⓒ Using one word

Rewrite these sentences using one word instead of the phrases that are in heavy type:

1   The concert was **put off until another day**.
2   They left by the door marked **Way Out**.
3   The sky was **without a cloud**.
4   Ann had **great numbers of** friends.
5   John **made up his mind** to win the prize.

Ⓓ Opposites

The opposite of **come** is **go**. Write out these sentences using the opposite of the word in heavy type to fill each space:

1   You must either **accept** or _______ the honour.
2   The valley was **near**; the mountainside was _______.
3   This sum is **easy**, but that one is _______.
4   They were led from **danger** to _______.
5   Do you come here **often**? No, very _______.

Ⓔ Abbreviations

Write out in full the abbreviations (shortened forms) shown in these sentences:

1   He was out **lbw** playing for England at Lord's.
2   She ordered a **CD** on the **WWW**.
3   **HRH** the Prince of Wales may visit the headquarters of the **UN**.
4   The **DVD** about the moon landings was made with the help of **NASA**.

TEST 3

(A) Read through the following passage very carefully, and then answer the questions.

The Stream

The first rays of the rising sun awoke the sleeping flowers on the hillside. The pink rose-bay willow-herb, the scarlet poppy, and the convolvulus with its white bells all seemed to glance upwards and stir themselves for another day. The stream, too, seemed to rouse itself, and sparkle more brightly as it dashed towards the river in the valley below. The sedges in the shallows moved gently to and fro, and the water-weed took on new shapes in the sunlight.

The colony of moorhens in their reedy home knew that it was time to be out and about in search of food, fun and adventure. The chicks became more and more daring as time went on, and darted here, there and everywhere, whilst their mothers kept careful watch in case enemies, two-footed or four-footed, should try to harm them.

1. What was it that woke the sleeping flowers?
2. What flowers are named in the story?
3. Which of the plants has a bell-shaped flower?
4. To where was the stream dashing?
5. What happened to the water plants when the sun shone?
   (*a*) They died from the heat. (*b*) They took on new shapes.
   (*c*) They went back to sleep.
6. Who lived in the reeds?
7. What three things might the moorhens look for?
8. How did the chicks behave as the day went on?
9. What were their mothers doing at this time?
10. What kinds of enemies were feared: (*a*) animals only;
    (*b*) humans only; (*c*) animals and human beings?

11 Write down, from this list, the words that describe the young hens: brave, high-spirited, cowardly, timid, daring, careful, fearless.

(B) Word-doubles

We call **one and only** a word-double.
Example: *He is the **one and only** champion.*
Complete these sentences with the correct word-doubles:

1 They fought back **time and** ______.
2 The car went by **fits and** ______.
3 Brian stood **head and** ______ above his friends.
4 Everything must be **spick and** ______ before the bell goes.

(C) Put in order

Here are five sentences from a story, but they are not in the order in which things happened. Write them in the correct order

1 It was very heavy.
2 As Jane walked along she saw a parcel in the gutter.
3 She took it to the police station.
4 She stooped to pick it up.
5 It was placed in a special cupboard.

(D) Gender

HE is a **masculine** word. Its partner SHE is a **feminine** word. In the following sentences, write **feminine** words in place of the **masculine** words shown in heavy type.

1 The **emperor** helped the **prince.**
2 The **husband** saw the **gentleman** to the door.
3 The **actor** is a **bachelor.**
4 **Sir, he** is a **traitor.**

(E) Punctuation

Punctuation marks (. , ? etc.) have been omitted from the following sentences. Rewrite the sentences correctly.

1 good morning said the girl
2 have you a belt the man asked
3 did you see lions tigers elephants and apes at the zoo
4 its a boundary cried the boy

TEST 4

(A) Read through the following passage very carefully, and then answer the questions.

On the Desert Island

Two sailors named Pat and Mike fell overboard from a ship, but managed to swim to an island. They roamed about in search of human beings, but found that the island was uninhabited. There wasn't even a hut where they could shelter for the night, so they lay down in the shade of a palm-tree, and were soon fast asleep.

After some time, however, they were awakened by swarms of mosquitoes, which came from a nearby lake. These ferocious insects bit them so much that sleep was out of the question. 'Let's pull our coats over our heads, and perhaps they'll go away,' Pat suggested.

They did so, and for some time all went well until Mike, being curious, looked out and saw some fireflies hovering overhead. 'It's no use hiding any longer, Pat,' he cried, 'they're looking for us with lanterns!'

1   How was it that the men were on the island?
2   What did they first try to find?
3   What did they do when they found their search was useless?
4   Write down the sentences that are true: (*a*) They slept until dawn next day. (*b*) They heard the roaring of lions. (*c*) They were awakened immediately. (*d*) They awoke some hours later. (*e*) Their sleep was disturbed by cannibals. (*f*) Fierce, stinging insects awoke them.
5   What did Pat suggest was a way of getting to sleep?
6   Why did Mike look out: (*a*) because he wanted something to eat; (*b*) because he had forgotten to wind the alarm-clock; (*c*) because he was curious as to what was going on?
7   What did Mike see when he looked out?
8   What did he believe was happening?

(B) Odd one out

In each of the following groups of words, one is out of place because it has nothing to do with the others. Write down the odd one out.
Example: *oak, ash, **banana**, elm.*

Banana is the odd one out because it is a fruit, and the other three are trees.

Find the odd one out in these:

1 Jennifer, Mary, Francis, Jane
2 pansy, marigold, violet, tulip
3 hut, caravan, bungalow, house
4 bus, sedan-chair, car, taxi

(C) This is to that

Example: **Sailor** *is to* **navy** *as* **soldier** *is to* **army**.
Now complete these:

1 **Fingers** are to **man** as _______ are to **lion**.
2 **Cup** is to **saucer** as **knife** is to _______.
3 **Walk** is to **legs** as **fly** is to _______.
4 **Radio** is to **ear** as **television** is to _______.

(D) Crossword puzzles

Here are some crossword-puzzle clues, and a part of each answer. Complete the words.

1 A plank of wood.   B _ _ _ D
2 Not expensive.   CH _ _ P
3 Rough and unpolished.   C _ _ RSE
4 To pretend to make an attack,   F _ INT
   as in a boxing match.

(E) Answer the questions

Write down the answers to the following questions.

1 What would you expect to find in a scabbard?
2 What is a place called where grapes are grown?
3 What is the work of a doctor?
4 On what would one play the game of football?
5 To what kind of shop should I go to buy bread?

TEST 5

(A) Read through the following verses very carefully, and then answer the questions.

Sir Ralph the Rover

Sir Ralph the Rover sailed away,
He scoured the sea for many a day;
And now grown rich with plundered store,
He steers his course for Scotland's shore.

So thick a haze o'erspreads the sky,
They cannot see the sun on high;
The wind has blown a gale all day,
At evening it hath died away.

On the deck the Rover takes his stand,
So dark it is they see no land.
Quoth Sir Ralph, 'It will be lighter soon,
For there is the dawn of the rising moon.'

Robert Southey

1 Sir Ralph was: (*a*) a peaceful trader; (*b*) a merchantman;
(*c*) a pirate; (*d*) an explorer?
2 How do we know that he had made a long voyage?
3 How can we tell that the weather was foggy?
4 What had the weather been like during the day?
5 Was Sir Ralph: (*a*) up the mainmast; (*b*) in the crow's nest;
(*c*) below; (*d*) standing on deck; (*e*) climbing the rigging?
6 What was he hoping to see?
7 Sir Ralph was making his way: (*a*) towards Scotland; (*b*) to
the South Seas; (*c*) up a river?
8 Why was it going to be lighter soon: (*a*) because they were
going to light a lantern; (*b*) because the sun was coming up;
(*c*) because the moon was rising?
9 What words or phrases in the story mean: (*a*) wanderer;
(*b*) passed swiftly over; (*c*) mist; (*d*) covers; (*e*) said?

ⓑ Common phrases

When we say that we have '*nipped something in the bud*' we mean that we have put an end to something before it becomes serious. 'Nipped in the bud' is a common phrase.

In the following, choose the words that mean nearly the same as the common phrase.

1 **To weigh anchor** means: (*a*) the way into a harbour; (*b*) to find the weight of a ship's anchor; (*c*) to haul up an anchor before setting sail.

2 **To bury the hatchet** means: (*a*) to make peace; (*b*) to hide an axe in the woodshed; (*c*) to have a funeral.

3 **A leap in the dark** means: (*a*) to go into a dark room; (*b*) to do something without having thought very carefully about it; (*c*) to take part in a high-jump competition at night.

ⓒ Sound-words

These are words that when spoken aloud give you some idea of their meaning. Choose suitable words to fill the spaces.

As the _______ of the drum stopped, the door _______, and the _______ of a cane was heard above the _______ of the clock.

ⓓ Alphabetical order

Here are the names of some famous football teams. Write them in alphabetical order.

Real Madrid, Barcelona, Arsenal, Tottenham, Juventus, Chelsea, Liverpool, Manchester United, Manchester City, Inter Milan.

ⓔ Nouns and adjectives

1 Here are four **nouns**: hill, cat, result, voice.

   And here are four **adjectives**, words that describe them: gruff, sleek, correct, steep.

   Write the words together in suitable pairs.

2 Here are four other **adjectives**: handsome, painful, plentiful, foaming.
   Here are four **nouns**: torrent, prince, supply, illness.

   Write them together in suitable pairs.

TEST 6

(A) Read through the following passage very carefully, and then answer the questions.

King Alfred

A long time ago an English king called Alfred, defeated by the Danes and separated from his army, had taken refuge in the hut of a cow-herd. The peasant and his wife did not know that the poor, hungry traveller was their king, and the woman had told him to keep an eye on some cakes that were baking at the side of the open fire.

It seems that Alfred, deep in thought as to how he could defeat his enemies, forgot about the cakes, and when the peasant-woman came back from the cow-byre, there they were, each burnt to a cinder. He was soundly scolded by the angry woman. But all ended well when some of Alfred's nobles came upon the scene and told her that the careless visitor was the king.

1 Why had Alfred taken refuge in the hut?
2 Which of these might the cowherd and his wife have said?
   (*a*) 'What do you want, stranger?' (*b*) 'Welcome, your Majesty, to our hut.' (*c*) 'Would you like to rest for a while until your generals come along?'
3 What special job was Alfred given to do?
4 Why did Alfred fail to do his job properly?
5 How did the woman show her anger?
6 How did she find out who her visitor was?
7 Write down the sentences that are true: (*a*) The cakes were laid on the hearth near the fire. (*b*) They were in separate tins in the oven. (*c*) They were burned because the gas was turned up too high. (*d*) They were burned because Alfred forgot to watch them. (*e*) The cakes were being cooked over the fire.
8 What words or phrases in the story mean: (*a*) had gone to safety; (*b*) a man who looks after cows; (*c*) the barn?

(B) Homophones

Some words have a similar sound, but are spelt differently.

Example: '*The cat's* **paws**', and '*There was a moment's* **pause**'.

In the sentences below, choose the correct word from those inside the brackets.

1   Joan of Arc was burned at the (**stake**, **steak**).
2   The bride and bridegroom walked down the (**isle**, **aisle**).
3   The wine was stored in a dark (**seller**, **cellar**).
4   He made the parcel secure with (**ceiling**, **sealing**) wax.

(C) Rhyming words

In and **pin** are rhyming words because they have the same sound. Write these twelve words in pairs, so that they rhyme:

beer	gnash	gaol	psalm	caught	calm
pail	brought	crash	draught	pier	raft

(D) Synonyms

Look at the word **small**. Now look at the three words inside the brackets (great, little, wise). The word nearest in meaning to **small** is **little**.

Do the same with these, choosing one word from inside the brackets each time:

1   **buy** (lose, purchase, lend)
2   **proud** (haughty, mean, careless)
3   **reveal** (hide, show, buy)
4   **pedestrian** (cyclist, airman, walker)

(E) Choose the correct word

Look at the word BIRD. A bird need not be **large**. It need not be able to **fly**, but it must have **wings**.

Choose one word from those in the brackets that always has to do with the word before the bracket:

1   **racket**   (press, strings, guarantee)
2   **watch**   (chain, face, strap)
3   **school**   (tower, playing-fields, pupils)
4   **knife**   (blade, silver, sheath)

TEST 7

(A) Read through the following passage very carefully, and then answer the questions.

The Ant and the Dove

Once, an ant who had come to drink at a stream fell into the water and was carried away by the swift current. He was in great danger of drowning. A dove, perched on a nearby tree, saw the ant's peril and dropped a leaf into the water. The ant clambered on to this, and was carried to safety.

Some time after this, a hunter, creeping through the bushes, spied the dove asleep, and took careful aim with his musket. He was about to fire when the ant, who was near by, crawled forward and bit him sharply in the ankle. The hunter missed his aim, and the loud report of the gun awakened the dove from her sleep. She saw her danger and flew swiftly away to safety. Thus the ant repaid the dove for having saved his life in the foaming current of the stream.

1 What brought the ant to the stream?
2 Where was the dove at that moment?
3 What was it that made a lifeboat for the ant?
4 Why was the dove in danger?
5 How did the ant startle the hunter?
6 What was the huntsman armed with: (*a*) a bow and arrow; (*b*) a spear; (*c*) a kind of gun; (*d*) a net?
7 The ant was in danger because: (*a*) the current was flowing swiftly; (*b*) it had struck its head; (*c*) the dove was seeking to kill it; (*d*) the bridge had broken down?
8 From this list choose words and phrases that describe the ant in the water: tiny, struggling, swimming contentedly, at his last gasp, at ease, given up for lost.

B **Put in order**

The words in each of the following are in the wrong order. Rearrange them to make sentences. (There may be more than one answer in some cases.)

1 Stable the horse into put the.
2 Knife and your lend me fork.
3 Nail the strike hammer the with.
4 From the scent a sweet came bottle.

C **Crossword puzzles**

Each of the answers to the following crossword-puzzle clues begins with the letters SAL. Write down the words.

1 A person's wages. SAL _ _ _
2 A fish. SAL _ _ _
3 Can be made from fruit, or vegetables. SAL _ _
4 Used to season your food. SAL _
5 Goods recovered after damage. SAL _ _ _ _

D **Homonyms**

The word **ball** has more than one meaning. It may mean 'a grand dance'; or it may mean 'a round object often used in games'.

Write down the words that fit in with the following descriptions.

1 A web-footed bird; to lower one's head quickly; a score of no runs at cricket.
2 To hit something; to stop work, and refuse to go back.
3 A piece of wood in the ground; to send a letter.
4 Something tied in a rope or string; a mark in wood.
5 The bottom of a shoe; a flat-fish; the only one.

E **Rhyming words**

Choose, from the words in brackets, the most suitable word to finish the line of poetry:

> We are three Lords come out of Spain
> That we may court your daughter (**Ann, Jill, Jane**).
> My daughter Jane is far too young,
> And cannot bear your flattering (**voice, tongue, tone, speech**).
> The fairest one that we can see
> Is pretty Nancy. Come to (**Spain, dinner, me, us**).

TEST 8

(A) Read through the following passage very carefully, and then answer the questions.

Theras Looks On

Theras stopped before a shop which was open all along the front of it. What fun it was to see the man squatting at the wheel, and making a pot out of soft clay. The wheel, made of solid wood, no spokes, lay flat before him like a table, and all the while the potter kept whirling it, whirling it. Then he slapped down a handful of clay on the middle of the wheel, and smoothed the whirling mass into a round shape. With both hands the potter pressed its sides, and it grew tall; then he put his fist in the middle, and it grew hollow. All the time it quivered and trembled. The clay certainly seemed alive. Already it had a base, and a pretty slender neck. Then the man squeezed it boldly, and with one more touch it changed into a pitcher. Surely that was magic.

C. D. Snedeker

1 What type of window made the shop different from the other shops: (*a*) double windows; (*b*) no windows; (*c*) stained-glass windows; (*d*) circular windows?

2 What was the man inside the shop making?

3 How do we know that he was not sitting down to his work?

4 What material was he using: (*a*) plasticine; (*b*) plywood; (*c*) raffia; (*d*) balsa wood; (*e*) clay?

5 When the worker pressed the sides, what happened? (*a*) The object grew taller. (*b*) It collapsed. (*c*) It changed colour. (*d*) It disappeared.

6 What made the clay seem to be alive? (*a*) It made a noise. (*b*) It changed its shape so quickly. (*c*) It had limbs like a human being.

7 This all seemed magic to Theras because: (*a*) the worker kept on saying magic words; (*b*) the clay kept on taking fresh shapes; (*c*) the man really was a magician.

8 Write down the sentences that are true: (*a*) The wheel had a number of spokes. (*b*) Theras was happy at what he saw.

(*c*) The workman had someone to help him. (*d*) The wheel was quite solid. (*e*) The man was a marvellous craftsman.

B Synonyms

The three words in the first brackets have similar meanings. Choose one word from those in the second brackets that is similar in meaning to those in the first brackets.

Example: (***look***, ***see***, ***observe***) – (*taste*, ***behold***, *follow*)

1   (request, ask, beg) – (crave, give, know)
2   (weak, feeble, delicate) – (powerful, frail, strong)
3   (folk, people, persons) – (humans, things, objects)
4   (doctor, surgeon, specialist) – (miner, grocer, physician)

C A or an?

We speak of **a** girl and **a** street, but **an** egg and **an** orange. Write **a** or **an** in the spaces in the following sentences.

1   _______ old man and _______ young man travelled in _______ new train.
2   Lend me _______ anorak instead of _______ shirt.
3   Here's _______ ticket for _______ exhibition.
4   _______ piece of toast and _______ egg make _______ appetizing meal.

D Proverbs

Complete these proverbs, or well-known sayings:

1   Two heads are better _______ _______.
2   A stitch in time _______ _______.
3   All's well _______ _______ _______.
4   Better late _______ _______.

E Proper nouns

Rewrite this paragraph, beginning each proper noun with a capital letter:

Long ago robin hood and his men lived in sherwood forest, near the town of nottingham. In those days you would have seen his friends friar tuck and little john in the greenwood. Once, king richard the lion-heart visited the robbers' camp, which was a long way from london.

TEST 9

(A) Read through the following passage very carefully, and then answer the questions.

The Thames

The River Thames rises in the Cotswold hills and flows in a south-easterly direction. On its way to the sea it passes through many well-known places, including Oxford, Windsor and Richmond. Every year one of the most famous races in the world takes place on its waters – the Oxford and Cambridge university boat race. The race starts at Putney and ends at Mortlake. The length of the course is 7.24 kilometres.

The Thames flows through the counties of Gloucestershire, Oxfordshire, Berkshire, Buckinghamshire, Middlesex, Surrey, Kent and Essex. It flows through lovely countryside and past world-famous buildings such as Hampton Court, Windsor Castle, the Houses of Parliament and the Tower of London. In olden times, the Thames was the main highway through London. Queen Elizabeth I was often rowed upon it in her State Barge. Then there were no stone embankments, and London Bridge was the only bridge.

1   In what hills does the Thames rise?
2   In what direction does it flow?
3   Name three well-known places through which it passes.
4   (*a*) Where does the boat race begin? (*b*) Where does it end?
    (*c*) How long is the course? (*d*) Who takes part in this race?
5   Name the counties through which the Thames flows.
6   'It was the main highway through London.' Does this mean:
    (*a*) the Thames was higher than it is today; (*b*) it flowed
    through pipes, like a water-main; (*c*) it was the easiest way to
    travel through London?
7   Under which of these bridges did Queen Elizabeth I pass:
    (*a*) Tower Bridge; (*b*) Westminster Bridge; (*c*) London Bridge;
    (*d*) Waterloo Bridge?

8 Write down the sentences that are true: (*a*) The State Barge could not move when the wind was not blowing. (*b*) Everyone could use the State Barge. (*c*) The State Barge belonged to the Queen. (*d*) The State Barge was propelled by oars. (*e*) The Royal Coach of today does the same job as the State Barge did then. (*f*) Queen Elizabeth I rowed the State Barge.

(B) Synonyms

From the words inside the brackets in each sentence, write down the one word that is nearest in meaning to the word in heavy type
Example: ***refuge***. *They took (dinner, **shelter**, root) in the hut.*

1	**innocent**	John is (guilty, blameless, careless).
2	**contented**	He was always a (disturbed, happy, restless) baby.
3	**protect**	The dog will (annoy, chase, guard) the flock.
4	**prompt**	Please send me a (careful, speedy, lengthy) reply.

(C) Word groups

Peas, beans, carrots and turnips are all **vegetables**. Write down one word that describes each of these groups:

1 pepper, mustard, salt, vinegar
2 tea, coffee, sugar, flour
3 football, tennis, cricket, hockey
4 bracelet, earrings, necklace, brooch
5 tiger, lion, panther, puma

(D) Put in order

Write these in order of size, beginning with the smallest:

1 sentence, letter, paragraph, chapter
2 dessert spoon, coffee spoon, teaspoon, tablespoon
3 turnip, marrow, pea, onion
4 pigeon, thrush, swan, wren

(E) Anagrams

Rearrange the letters of the words below to make the name of a fruit.
Example: *CHEAP becomes PEACH.*

1 PLEAP   3 ANABAN
2 RREYCH   4 PAGRE

TEST 10

(A) Read through the following verses very carefully, and then answer the questions.

The Pigtail

There lived a sage in days of yore,
And he a handsome pigtail wore,
But wondered much, and sorrowed more,
Because it hung behind him.

He mused upon this curious case,
And swore he'd change the pigtail's place,
And have it hanging at his face,
Not dangling there behind him.

Said he, 'The mystery I've found;
I'll turn me round.' – He turned him round:
But still it hung behind him.

W. M. Thackeray

1 Write down the four words that tell us that this was happening some time ago.
2 What was worrying the man in the story: (*a*) that his eyesight was failing him; (*b*) that his hair was getting thin; (*c*) that his cheeks had grown pale; (*d*) that his pigtail was hanging at the back of him?
3 What was he trying so hard to do?
4 How did he think that he would be able to do this?
5 Write the line that tells us that he did not succeed in doing so.
6 A sage is: (*a*) a person who grows herbs in a garden; (*b*) a person who drives a coach; (*c*) a wise and learned person; (*d*) a person who lives amongst the sage-bushes in the garden?
7 Write down the words and phrases that describe the way in which the man was behaving: foolishly, wisely, in an extra-ordinary way, in an unusual way, in a peculiar way, happily.
8 Write in full: I've, I'll.

Ⓑ Capital letters

Read through this passage very carefully, and then write it down as it should be written, in verse. Begin each new line with a capital letter.

Gaily bedight, a gallant knight, in sunshine and in shadow, had journeyed long, singing a song, in search of El Dorado.

Ⓒ Word ladder

Beginning with the word BAD, and changing only one letter at a time, we can make the word COT.

Example: *BAD, CAD, CAT, COT.*

In the same way, change the word HARD into the word EASY.

HARD

1	One of a pack of 52.	_ _ _ _
2	We drive a horse and	_ _ _ _
3	To throw (a stone?)	_ _ _ _
4	Opposite of west.	_ _ _ _

EASY

Ⓓ Lists

Look at this:

Country – *France*   **People** – *French*   **Language** – *French*

Now complete these lists:

	Country	**People**	**Language**
1	England		
2	China		
3	Sweden		
4	Italy		

Ⓔ Who are these characters?

Name these people of whom we read in books:

1 He was an outlaw who lived in Sherwood Forest.
2 He was taught at a wizarding school.
3 He was stranded on a desert island.
4 He was a very mean man, especially at Christmas-time.
5 She fell down a rabbit-hole.
6 He was a boy who could fly.

TEST 11

(A) Read through the following passage very carefully, and then answer the questions.

The Village Shop

Our local shop sold an astonishing number of things. You could buy almost anything you wanted there from bootlaces to bull's-eyes, from tea cosies to corn-cure. If the object we wanted didn't happen to be in stock, without hesitation the shopkeeper would say, 'I can get it for you.' We often wondered if she would say this if we asked for an elephant, or a king's crown. We were too scared to put this to the test.

On one occasion one of the local boys, because of the slow way in which the shop was run, fastened a tortoise to the front door as a hint to the proprietor. But the shopkeeper took not the slightest notice of this, and carried on as usual, moving in her careful manner from one customer to another, enquiring about each one's illness, or how the children were getting on at school.

1 Write down the sentences that are true: (*a*) The shop sold objects of one kind only. (*b*) The shop was situated in a large town. (*c*) The shopkeeper rushed madly from one part of the shop to another. (*d*) It was almost certain that the shop had what you wanted. (*e*) Within the shop it was peaceful.
2 Write down the names of the four things mentioned as being in stock.
3 What were the two unusual things for which we thought of asking?
4 What did the shopkeeper say if an object was out of stock?
5 How did one of the local boys show that he was not satisfied?
6 What effect did this have on the shopkeeper?
7 In what two things was the shopkeeper interested when she spoke to customers?
8 Divide the words below into two lists: (*a*) those that describe the local boy, and (*b*) those that describe the shopkeeper: calm, playful, impatient, restless, quiet, kindly, comical, tender-hearted, placid, humorous.

B Choose the correct word

A **splinter** is **a very small piece of wood**. Here are some other small amounts:

scrap   drop   pinch   speck

Choose the correct ones to use with these words:

salt   dirt   rain   paper

C Joining words

Below are pairs of sentences. Join each pair by using one of the following words: **which**, **who**, **when**, **where**. You may have to omit some of the words in some cases.

1. John will go to Brighton. He will meet his friend.
2. Everyone has heard of Wellington. He was the hero of Waterloo.
3. He had begun shouting. The police came in.
4. St Paul's is a famous cathedral in London. It was built by Wren.

D Word endings

Complete the words below by adding **ery** or **ary**, whichever is correct.

1. John went to read the books in the **libr** _______.
2. The ball was lost in the **shrubb** _______.
3. The funeral went on its way to the **cemet** _______.
4. On the edge of the moor stood a **solit** _______ cottage.

E Past tense

Below is a story. The words in heavy type show that it is taking place **now**. Change these words so that the story happened **in the past**.

The coach **draws** up at the inn, and the only passenger **dismounts**. He **gives** his coat a shake, and then **passes** into the dining-room, where a fire **burns** in the grate, and hot coffee **awaits** him. The coach **goes** on its way, and the innkeeper **stares** after it.

TEST 12

(A) Read through the following passage very carefully, and then answer the questions.

The Frogs

Some frogs who lived in a large pond wished very much to have a king to rule over them, but they could not decide which of them should be chosen. So they asked Jupiter, the king of the gods, to send them a king. Jupiter, saying 'This is your king', dropped a heavy log, with a great splash, into the pool. After a time the frogs grew used to the log, which only floated there and did nothing else. So they asked Jupiter for a new king, one who would be more exciting.

This time Jupiter sent them a stork to rule over them, and it was not long before the new king was moving about amongst his subjects, gobbling up as many as he could catch. The frogs fled in terror to the bottom of the pool. They asked Jupiter to take away their cruel king. But Jupiter refused to do so.

1. (*a*) Where did the frogs live? (*b*) What did they wish for?
2. Why didn't they choose a frog for a king?
3. Who was Jupiter?
4. How did King Log show that he had arrived?
5. Why were the frogs not satisfied with the log as a king?
6. The second king was: (*a*) a lifeless object; (*b*) a human being; (*c*) a live creature?
7. How did the stork show that he was the master of the frogs?
8. Where did the frogs take refuge?
9. What did the frogs then ask Jupiter to do?
10. Write down the statements that are true: (*a*) The frogs were peaceful and contented. (*b*) They were always wanting something different. (*c*) They lived in a swift-flowing river. (*d*) Jupiter helped them each time they asked him to. (*e*) The stork was a merciless ruler.

Ⓑ Apostrophes

Look at this sentence: Where is **Jims** ball? The **apostrophe** is missing. The sentence should be: Where is **Jim's** ball?

Put the apostrophe in its correct place in each of the following sentences.

1 This is Bettys doll.
2 Have you read 'King Solomons Mines'?
3 You have spoilt the childs game.
4 You have spoilt the childrens game.
5 Are you the boys (more than one) mother?

Ⓒ Speech

Look at these two sentences:

a Alice asked: 'Where is it?'
b Alice asked where it was.

In the first sentence Alice **speaks the words**. In the second sentence she does not actually speak. Change the following sentences so that the people are **actually speaking**.

1 The boy said that he was afraid.
2 The crowd shouted that it was a goal.
3 The girl said that she was eleven.
4 The explorer said that he was lost.

Ⓓ Word-doubles

When we hear the word **collar** we often think of the word **tie**. Write down the words that go with the following.

1 Shoes and ______
2 Bat and ______
3 Left and ______
4 Bucket and ______
5 Arms and ______
6 Pen and ______

Ⓔ Using one word

Each of the following words begins with **ph** that sounds as **f**.

1 King in ancient Egypt.
2 A ghost, or shadowy creature.
3 A group of words, not a sentence.
4 A person who takes pictures.

TEST 13

(A) Read through the following passage very carefully, and then answer the questions.

The Journey

We wended our way back to the coast, intending to encamp near the beach, for the mosquitoes were troublesome in the forest. We could not help admiring the birds which flew and chirped around us. Among them we observed a pretty kind of parakeet with a green body and a blue head, a few beautiful turtle doves, and several flocks of wood pigeons. The hues of many of these birds were very vivid – bright green, blue and scarlet. We made several attempts to bring down one of the birds, both with the bow and sling, to find out whether they were good for food. But we always missed, although once or twice we were very near hitting.

As evening drew on, however, a flock of pigeons flew past. I slung a stone into the midst of them, and had the good fortune to hit one.

R. M. Ballantyne

1 Why did they wish to encamp near the beach, and not in the forest?
2 Write down the sentences that are true: (*a*) They hurried back. (*b*) They strolled back. (*c*) They hastened back. (*d*) They ran back. (*e*) They wandered back. (*f*) They rode back. (*g*) They ambled back.
3 What birds did they see whilst returning?
4 Which of these are correct? (*a*) The birds were plain in colour. (*b*) The birds were brightly coloured. (*c*) The birds' feathers were dazzling. (*d*) There was nothing very striking about the birds. (*e*) They took no notice of the birds. (*f*) They looked with interest at the birds.
5 What did they make several attempts to do?
6 How do we know that they were not successful?
7 They did not succeed because: (*a*) the gun did not fire; (*b*) the arrows flew wide; (*c*) the spear was too short; (*d*) the stone missed

its target; (*e*) there was a hole in the net; (*f*) their aim was not good enough; (*g*) the birds were too difficult to hit?

8 When they brought down a pigeon, how do we know that they were not aiming at any particular pigeon?

9 Which words or phrases mean: (*a*) saw, or noticed; (*b*) colours; (*c*) a bird of the parrot family; (*d*) tries; (*e*) the middle?

(B) **Where do they live?**

You might find a **family** in a **house**. Where might you find these people?

1	An Inuit	**3**	A soldier	**5**	A tourist
2	A king	**4**	A convict	**6**	A chef

(C) **Choose the correct word**

Rewrite the paragraph below, using a word from the list given to fill each of the spaces.

fro	white-sailed	valley	river
sun	together	babbling	sea

The _______ stream rippled through the _______ until she met with her big sister, the _______. Then _______ they rushed towards the _______, where the _______ ships darted to and _______, and the water sparkled in the summer _______.

(D) **Comparative adjectives**

Jill's doll is **pretty**, Pat's is **prettier**, but Sally's is **prettiest**. Fill in the spaces in these sentences in the same way:

1 My share is **small**, your share is _______ , but his is the _______.

2 Norah was **clever**, Dora was _______, but Cora was the _______.

3 Tom lives **far** away, Dick lives _______, and Harry lives _______.

4 My hair is **dark**, Judith's is _______, and Janet's is _______.

(E) **Sound-words**

Fill in the spaces below with the correct sound-words:

Can you tell the difference between the _______ of a lion and the _______ of a wolf, or the _______ of a seagull and the _______ of a pigeon? We all know that a cat _______ when happy, and _______ when unhappy.

TEST 14

(A) Read through the following passage very carefully, and then answer the questions.

Long, Long Ago

A long time ago the island of Britain was joined to the rest of Europe, and hills and forests once stood where the North Sea and the English Channel are today. Then, owing to some great earthquakes, much of the land sank, the sea rushed in, and only the high parts remained above the surface of the water. Before this happened the mountains of Britain – Ben Nevis, Snowdon and others – must have been very high land indeed.

How do we know all this? Fishermen trawling in the North Sea and the English Channel have found in their nets the bones of prehistoric animals that must have been roaming about on what was once dry land. Sabre-toothed tigers, mammoths and other creatures that disappeared long, long ago could not have been paddling about in canoes, could they?

1 What used to be where the North Sea and the English Channel are today?
2 What caused much of the land to sink?
3 Which two mountains are named in the story?
4 We know all this is true, because: (*a*) it was written down in books at that time; (*b*) it was told by father to son; (*c*) the bones of dry-land animals have been brought to the surface by fishermen?
5 Which two prehistoric animals are named in the story?
6 When did all this happen: (*a*) last year; (*b*) during the last century; (*c*) in the last five hundred years; (*d*) thousands of years ago?
7 Why were the bones of these animals found by trawling fishermen: (*a*) because trawl nets scrape along the seabed; (*b*) because trawlers are the only kind of fishing-boat; (*c*) because they use divers to go down to the seabed?

8   Sabre-toothed tigers and mammoths are prehistoric animals. Does this mean: (*a*) they are still roaming about today in all countries; (*b*) they once lived, but died out thousands of years ago; (*c*) there never were such animals?

(B) What are they?

A young **wolf** is a **cub**. Write down the names for the young of the animals and people listed below:

1	dog	**3**	hen	**5**	swan
2	fox	**4**	cat	**6**	king

(C) Adjectives

From the word **strong** (*The man was strong*), we can make the word **strength** (*The man had great strength*).

In the same way, rewrite the sentences below, changing the word given before each and putting it in the space.

1 **proud**   She showed great _______ in her work.
2 **angry**   You must not show your _______ at what he has done.
3 **brave**   She was praised for her _______.
4 **clean**   The visitor noticed the _______ of the streets.

(D) Adverbs

Here are six words that describe **how** something is done:

gracefully	sweetly	swiftly
bravely	peacefully	quietly

Use one of the words in each of the following sentences:

1	He slept _______.	**4**	They fought _______.	
2	She danced _______.	**5**	He hummed _______.	
3	They sang _______.	**6**	She ran _______.	

(E) Word groups

At what type of shop should I buy the following:

1	beds, chairs, tables	**3**	bulbs, plants, flowers
2	pumps, tyres, inner-tubes	**4**	sausages, mince, chops

TEST 15

(A) Read through the following verses very carefully, and then answer
the questions.

Hiawatha

Down a narrow pass they wandered,
Where a brooklet led them onward,
Where the trail of deer and bison
Marked the soft mud on the margin,
Till they found all further passage
Shut against them, barred securely
By the trunks of trees uprooted,
Lying lengthwise, lying crosswise,
And forbidding further passage.

'We must go back,' said the old man,
'O'er the logs we cannot clamber;
Not a woodchuck could get through them,
Not a squirrel clamber o'er them.'

H. W. Longfellow

1 Write down the sentences that are true: (*a*) They walked down
   a wide roadway. (*b*) The track was narrow and muddy.
   (*c*) A stream rippled near at hand. (*d*) The surface was hard
   and rocky. (*e*) A deep river flowed near by. (*f*) The people
   were going along quite slowly.
2 What stopped them from going further along the path?
3 How did they know that animals had been along there also?
4 How do we know that the trees had not been chopped down?
5 How did the old man say 'We cannot climb over these tree-
   trunks'?
6 Which line of the poem tells us that the trees were not all
   lying in the same direction?
7 What words or phrases mean: (*a*) a small brook; (*b*) the edge
   of the brook?

Ⓑ Forming adjectives

From the word **love** we can make the word **loving**.

Rewrite the sentences below, changing the word given before each and putting it in the space.

1 **sense** You are a very _______ person.
2 **pride** The _______ king sat on his throne.
3 **glory** It was a _______ victory.
4 **velvet** The mole has a _______ skin.

Ⓒ Who does what?

1 A **pedlar** (*a*) rides a bicycle; (*b*) sells things at people's houses; (*c*) interferes with other people.
2 A **jockey** (*a*) plays a card game; (*b*) rides horses; (*c*) repairs chimneys and high buildings.
3 A **surgeon** (*a*) makes things out of serge; (*b*) performs operations; (*c*) catches fish.
4 A **chauffeur** (*a*) drives a private car; (*b*) does no work at all; (*c*) sells groceries.

Ⓓ Opposites

Look at these two words: **obey** and **disobey**. By adding **dis** to **obey** the word becomes the exact opposite in meaning.

Now write the opposites of these words, using **dis**, **un**, **im** or **in**: fair, possible, connect, visible, happy, mortal.

Ⓔ Choose the correct word

Look at these three words: **inform**, **perform**, **reform**. Which of them would you write in the space in this sentence? *The doctor is going to _______ an operation.* Answer: **perform**.

Fill the gaps in these sentences, choosing one word each time:

1 **cataract, parapet, minaret**. The canoe was washed over the _______.
2 **complete, compete, consult**. Shall we _______ in the game?
3 **department, compartment, appointment**. There were three empty seats in the next _______ of the train.

TEST 16

(A) Read through the following passage very carefully, and then answer the questions.

The Tea-Party

There was a table set out under a tree in front of the house, and the March Hare and the Hatter were having tea at it. A Dormouse was sitting, between them, fast asleep, and the other two were using it as a cushion, resting their elbows on it, and talking over its head. 'Very uncomfortable for the Dormouse,' thought Alice, 'only, as it's asleep, I suppose it doesn't mind.'

The table was a large one, but the three were all crowded together at one corner of it. 'No room! No room!' they cried together when they saw Alice. 'There's **plenty** of room,' said Alice indignantly, as she sat down in a large arm-chair at one end of the table.

'Have some wine,' the March Hare said. Alice looked around the table, but there was nothing on it but tea.

'I don't see any wine,' she remarked.

Lewis Carroll

1   Where was the table placed: (*a*) out of doors; (*b*) in the kitchen; (*c*) in the dining-room; (*d*) on the tree?
2   When Alice arrived, who were already at the table?
3   What did they shout when they saw Alice?
4   What was Alice's reply?
5   What did the March Hare offer Alice to drink: (*a*) a cup of tea; (*b*) a mug of cocoa; (*c*) some wine; (*d*) a beaker of milk?
6   Why couldn't Alice accept the March Hare's offer?
7   The Dormouse was not very comfortable, but the others were. Why was this?
8   Why didn't the Dormouse seem to mind?
9   Why is the word **plenty** printed differently from the other words?
10 Which of these words describe Alice at that point: cross, pleased, irritated, delighted, dissatisfied, annoyed, vexed, charmed, happy, displeased?

(B) Word groups

Chairs, benches, stools, forms, are all **seats**. Write down a general name for each of these groups:

1 gull, puffin, tern, guillemot
2 ant, bee, wasp, fly
3 London, Paris, Brussels, Madrid
4 euro, dollar, rupee, yen
5 BBC, PTO, lbw, DVD

(C) Past tense

Below is a paragraph. The words in heavy type show that the story is taking place **now**. Change these words so that the story happened **in the past**.

The school party **leaves** the station and **makes** its way down the road. As the children **see** the inviting sea they **shout** for joy and **hurry** to the beach as fast as they **can**. The day **is** hot and they **are** keen to have a swim.

(D) Forming nouns

From the word **lose** we can make the word **loss**.

Rewrite the sentences below, changing the word given before each sentence and putting it in the space.

1 **obey** I must have complete _______ from you all.
2 **invent** The telephone is a wonderful _______.
3 **succeed** I look forward to hearing of your _______.
4 **describe** This is a _______ of what I saw.

(E) Choose the correct word

Write **is** or **are** in the space in each sentence:

1 Each tyre _______ punctured.
2 Their brother and sister _______ away from school.
3 Both the chapter and the book _______ finished.
4 One of the panes _______ broken.

TEST 17

(A) Read through the following passage very carefully, and then answer the questions.

Books

John had one shelf in the bookcase for his own books. There were books of adventure and school stories, with brightly coloured covers. Most of the books contained exciting pictures of hunters fighting battles with hungry wolves or man-eating lions. Others showed spaceships circling the earth, linking up in space, or landing on strange planets.

John knew many of these stories by heart, for he had read them so many times. Yet, every evening he would take one down from the shelf and carry it away to his bedroom, to look at it just as eagerly as if it were a new book. Now and then there were new books to add to the shelf, and his proudest possession was the colourful encyclopaedia that he had been given for his birthday.

1   Where did John keep his books?
2   Which kinds of books did he like?
3   In what way were the book covers similar?
4   Write down the sentences that are true. The pictures in most of the books were: (*a*) of airmen flying over deserts; (*b*) of fights between hunters and animals; (*c*) of people playing basketball; (*d*) of spaceships and strange planets; (*e*) of famous buildings; (*f*) of people washing up after dinner.
5   How can we tell that John knew the contents of many of the books very well?
6   How often did he add new books to his shelf?
7   What was John's proudest possession?
8   John looked at the book 'eagerly'. Write down the words and phrases from this list that have a similar meaning to eagerly: calmly, shocked, coolly, breathlessly, without much interest, excitedly.

B Similes

When speaking of something **hard**, we may say it is **as hard as iron**.

Choose the correct answers from these:

1 As quick as: (*a*) a smash; (*b*) a flash; (*c*) a splash.
2 As slow as: (*a*) a tortoise; (*b*) a bus; (*c*) a noise.
3 As busy as: (*a*) a wasp; (*b*) a bee; (*c*) a hen.
4 As keen as: (*a*) custard; (*b*) mustard; (*c*) marbles.

C Compound words

Here are two words, **table** and **spoon**. From these we can make the word **tablespoon**.

From these eight words make four new compound words:

fire	north	wash	fighter
water	basin	west	colour

D Complete the story

Rewrite the paragraph below, using a word from the list to fill each of the spaces:

horses	eagerly	money	carved
purses	fair	favourite	left

At the _______, the roundabout with its galloping _______ was a great _______. The children _______ paid their _______ to ride, time after time, the bright, _______ animals, until there was no money _______ in their _______.

E Making new words

From the word **mock** (*He began to mock the old man*) we can make the word **mocking** (*He made a mocking sound*).

Now rewrite the sentences below, changing the word given before each and putting it in the space.

1 **study** She was a _______ student.
2 **enjoy** I hope you will have an _______ party.
3 **rebel** The soldiers are in a _______ mood.
4 **decide** The teacher gave the _______ vote.

TEST 18

(**A**) Read through the following passage very carefully, and then answer the questions.

The Rebels

The lone soldier leaped from the saddle and took refuge behind the pile of rocks at the edge of the road. None too soon for, already, shots were whistling around him, and the cries of the rebels were loud in his ears.

It would take all of 'Quickdraw' Thompson's courage and determination to get him safely out of this peril. Not only was his life at stake, but so were those of the townspeople sleeping peacefully in their log cabins in the lovely valley below. It was so long since there had been a rebel rising that the townspeople had become careless. Their guns were seldom to hand, and their look-outs had begun to think that they were wasting their time peering out across the fields for an enemy that never came. The rebels had chosen the time carefully. 'Bloody' Jackson had seen to that!

1 Who are the two most important people in the story?
2 Where did the soldier hide?
3 Why was he only just in time?
4 Why was Thompson named 'Quickdraw': (*a*) because he was clever at drawing pictures; (*b*) because he was quick at drawing his gun, and firing; (*c*) because he sometimes drew a truck loaded with goods?
5 Who were in danger from a rebel attack?
6 Say why 'Bloody' Jackson had chosen his time carefully.
7 Write down the one word that describes: (*a*) how the townspeople were sleeping; (*b*) the valley; (*c*) the noise of the shots.
8 What two words tell us that Thompson was a useful man to have nearby if you were in trouble?

(B) Collective nouns

A number of **chicks** together is called a **brood**. What words could
be used for:

1 A number of whales
2 A large number of locusts
3 A number of angels
4 A number of oxen drawing a wagon

(C) More than one

Rewrite these sentences so that they mean more than one.
Example: *The **card** lay in the **box**. The **cards** lay in the **boxes**.*

1 The child saw the fox.
2 She put the puppy in its basket.
3 The cook sharpened the knife.
4 The deer ate the loaf of bread.

(D) Spot the mistakes

There are mistakes in each of these sentences. Rewrite the sentences
correctly.

1 He is older than her.
2 Did you hear who ring the bell?
3 She read that poem quite loud.
4 The teacher sung the song at twelve o'clock.
5 The day had just began.

(E) Making new words

From the word **blood** (*The blood began to flow*) we can make the
word **bleed** (*He might bleed to death*). In the same way, rewrite the
sentences below, changing the word given before each and putting
it in the space.

1 **relief**   Let us try to _______ the army in the hills.
2 **thought**   Try to _______ harder about it.
3 **provision** It is up to us to _______ food for the old people.
4 **mystery**   The conjurer began to _______ his audience.

TEST 19

(A) Read through the following passage very carefully, and then answer the questions.

The Treasure Box

The ornamental box was taken from the cellar and placed in the centre of the table in the study. Jim's next task was to open the box. Try as he might, he could discover no keyhole, so it seemed clear that a spring of some sort would have to be found.

There were numerous decorations carved on the top and sides: grinning faces, baskets of fruit, sheaves of corn, any of which, when pressed, might cause a panel to slide, or a lid to spring open. There were many failures before Jim's searching fingers finally discovered the correct little carving. Silently, one side of the box collapsed and showed him the secret. There lay the roll of parchment about which so much had been written. It was the treasure-map, the clue to the vast hoard that was hidden somewhere else in the castle.

1   Where was the box: (*a*) upstairs, in the attic; (*b*) out in the garden; (*c*) below, in the cellar; (*d*) in a garden shed?
2   Where, and in what room, was it then placed?
3   What was Jim's next task?
4   What did he fail to find?
5   What were the carvings that decorated the box?
6   How might one of these carvings lead to the opening of the box?
7   How did the box finally open?
8   What was the secret found inside the box?
9   Why was this so valuable?
10   What words or phrases in the story mean: (*a*) bundles of corn; (*b*) noiselessly; (*c*) gave way; (*d*) decorative; (*e*) great collection?

11 Write down the sentences that are true: (*a*) Jim found the secret in a few seconds. (*b*) The secret was never discovered. (*c*) It was some time before Jim solved the problem. (*d*) The box was quite empty. (*e*) The box contained one thing only. (*f*) The lid of the box finally opened.

(B) Using one word

Rewrite these sentences using one word that means nearly the same as the phrases in heavy type:

1 The children **made fun of** the film.
2 The man was **without a hair on his head**.
3 Martin was **absolutely tired out** after the race.
4 Jane was **liked by everyone**.

(C) Opposites

The opposite of the word **in** is **out**. Write out these sentences, using the opposite of the word in heavy type to fill the space:

1 This park is **public**; that garden is ______.
2 What is the ______ to my **question**?
3 ______ is the opposite of **plural**.
4 You will have either **success** or ______ this time.

(D) Abbreviations and contractions

Write out in full the abbreviations (shortened forms) or contractions shown in these sentences:

1 The climbers reached the summit of **Mt** Everest.
2 The case was investigated by the **CIA**.
3 They bought the goods from Harris and **Co. Ltd**.
4 Her newspaper story was picked up by the **BBC**.

(E) Making new words

From the word **stolen** we can make the word **steal**.

Rewrite the sentences below, changing the word given before each and putting it in the space.

1 **decorative**   It is time to ______ the dining-room.
2 **strong**   It might be wise to ______ the wall.
3 **annoying**   Try not to ______ your brother.
4 **married**   The prince is going to ______ the peasant.

TEST 20

(A) Read through the following verses very carefully, and then answer the questions.

The Jolly Old Vagabond

One evening when Philip and I were out walking,
We saw in the forest the glow of a fire,
And somehow we knew it was best to stop talking
Whilst pushing through tangles of blackthorn and brier.

And as we drew near, the sound of a fiddle
Came stealing so gaily the branches among,
And there in a clearing, alone in the middle,
We saw someone jigging, and singing a song.

A jolly old man in a coat torn and tattered
Was bowing and scraping, so happy and gay;
His shirt was in ribbons, his hat bent and battered,
But he danced and he sang in a wonderful way.

1 At what time was all this taking place?
2 Why did the children think it was best to stop talking:
(*a*) because they knew there were wild animals about; (*b*) because
they were not quite certain what was happening; (*c*) because it
was getting near school-time?
3 How can we tell that it was difficult to reach the clearing?
4 Write down the sentences that are true: (*a*) They saw a band
of musicians practising. (*b*) The sound of a trumpet echoed
through the trees. (*c*) There was only one performer present.
(*d*) The player was in uniform. (*e*) There was an open space in
the forest. (*f*) He was a rather unusual person.
5 The man was doing two things besides playing the fiddle.
What were they?
6 Which words tell us that the man was performing 'very well
indeed'?

7   Look at the words 'stealing so gaily the branches among'.
Does this mean: (*a*) happily taking other people's goods;
(*b*) climbing through the trees like a squirrel; (*c*) sounding
so pleasantly through the trees?

(B) Word groups

Oak, ash, elm, chestnut are all **trees**. Give a general name for each
of the following groups.

1   lance, sword, cutlass, dagger
2   carnation, daisy, buttercup, lily
3   history, geography, arithmetic, science
4   barley, maize, wheat, oats
5   butter, eggs, cheese, cream

(C) Who are these characters?

Name these people of whom we read in books or poems:

1   She was helped by seven dwarfs.
2   He was a detective with an assistant called Dr Watson.
3   He was a bear who was very fond of honey.
4   She was awoken by a kiss from a prince.
5   He was a pirate, searching for gold, on Treasure Island.

(D) Complete the story

Rewrite the paragraph below, using a word from the list to fill each
of the spaces.

near   faithful   king   master   fondest   servant

An old ______ lay sick, and when he found his end was drawing
______, he said: 'Let ______ John come to me.' Now he was the
______ that the king was ______ of, and he was so called because
he had been true to his ______ all his life.

(E) Word-doubles

We call **high and low** a word-double.

Complete these sentences with the correct word-doubles:

1   The defenders fought **tooth and** ______ at the gates.
2   The attacking army fought with **might and** ______.
3   We must try to make a **rough and** ______ barrier.
4   They stood together through **thick and** ______.

TEST 21

(A) Read through the following passage very carefully, and then answer the questions.

Karl Katz

A great many years ago there lived in a village at the foot of a mountain a man called Karl Katz. Karl was a goatherd, and every morning he drove his flock to a part of the mountainside where there were patches of good grass. In the evenings, he sometimes thought it too late to drive his flock home, so he used to shut up the animals in a ruin in the woods. The ruin was part of an old castle that had long been deserted, and the walls were high enough to form a fold in which he could count his goats and let them rest for the night. One evening he found that the prettiest goat of his flock had vanished soon after they were driven into the fold. He searched for it everywhere, but in vain.

1   Karl Katz lived: (*a*) in a village on the mountain-top; (*b*) in a village half-way up a mountain; (*c*) in a village near the sea; (*d*) in a village at the foot of a mountain?

2   When did this story happen: (*a*) last year; (*b*) last week; (*c*) a very long time ago?

3   Karl was in charge of: (*a*) a flock of goats; (*b*) a herd of cows; (*c*) a flock of sheep; (*d*) a caravan of camels?

4   At what time of day did he drive his animals to feed?

5   What was the ready-made fold he found on the mountainside?

6   When did he sometimes use this place?

7   Which one of his flock was missing?

8   What did he do when he discovered his loss?

9   He drove his flock to certain places: (*a*) because they were near at hand; (*b*) because he was too lazy to go anywhere else; (*c*) because the best grass was to be found there?

10   What words or phrases in the story mean: (*a*) a place for keeping goats; (*b*) a number of goats; (*c*) disappeared; (*d*) without succeeding?

B Put in order

Here are five sentences from a story, but they are not in the order in which things happened. Write them in the correct order.

1 He tried hard to find the reason for the break.
2 There seemed to be nothing he could do.
3 In the middle of the programme, the radio stopped.
4 After a while he gave it up in despair.
5 David crossed over to the set.

C Gender

In the following sentences write **feminine** words in place of the **masculine** words shown in heavy type.

1 My **uncle** is my **landlord**.
2 My **brother** is a **waiter**.
3 The **monk** became an **abbot**.

D Punctuation

Punctuation marks (full stops, capital letters, commas, etc.) have been omitted from the following sentences. Rewrite the sentences correctly:

1 once upon a time there were a hare a rabbit and a tortoise
2 shes not tired at the moment
3 its not so much its shape as its size
4 thats not so

E Odd one out

In each of the following groups of words, one word is out of place because it has nothing to do with the others.

Example: *boy, girl, lass, woman, **tiger**.*

Tiger is the odd one out, because all the others are people.

Find the odd one out in these:

1 gaol, prison, goal, jail
2 father, mother, uncle, sister
3 tennis, football, ice-hockey, cricket
4 cycle, walk, tramp, march

TEST 22

(A) Read through the following passage very carefully, and then answer the questions.

Lost Property

It happened one day aboard the *Antelope* that Sam, the captain's servant, whilst emptying the captain's silver teapot, accidentally dropped the valuable article overboard. He was terrified as to what would happen when the captain found out, so he made up his mind to make things a little easier for himself.

'Sir, is a thing lost when you know where it is?' he asked the skipper.

'Of course it isn't,' was the reply. 'If you know where it is, it can't be lost.'

'Are you quite sure of that, sir?' Sam asked anxiously.

'As sure as I am that this ship is sailing the Pacific,' said the captain.

'Well, that makes me very happy indeed,' said Sam. 'Your silver teapot isn't really lost, for I know where it is. It's at the bottom of the ocean.'

1 What was the ship's name, and where was it at the time?
2 What was Sam's job aboard the vessel?
3 What is he doing when the story begins?
4 Write down the sentences that are true: (*a*) Sam was very light-hearted at what had happened. (*b*) He was very worried. (*c*) He went about whistling happily. (*d*) He had no fear of anything. (*e*) He was very much alarmed. (*f*) He was in a panic.
5 What was the first question he asked the captain?
6 Why did Sam repeat the question?
7 The captain's answers made Sam feel: pleased, happy, uneasy, light of heart, downhearted, disappointed, depressed. Write down the words or phrases that are true.

Ⓑ **This is to that**

Example: **_Soldier_** *is to* **army** *as* **sailor** *is to* **navy**.

Complete the rest of these sentences in this style:

1 **Oil** is to **well** as **coal** is to _______.
2 **Eleven** is to **cricket** as **fifteen** is to _______.
3 **I** is to **me** as **we** is to _______.
4 **Come** is to **go** as **here** is to _______.

Ⓒ **Crossword puzzles**

Give the answers to these crossword-puzzle clues:

1 To take a chance.   G _ MB _ _
2 Quietness.   P _ _ CE
3 A sound made in pain.   G _ _ _ N
4 A part of something.   P _ _ CE

Ⓓ **What are they?**

Write down the answers to the following questions.

1 What would you expect to find in a wardrobe?
2 Give the name of a place where many birds build their nests.
3 Where might you hear a cry of 'Fares, please!'?
4 What is the work of a carpenter?
5 Where would one play a game of football?
6 To what kind of shop should I go to buy a chisel?

Ⓔ **Common phrases**

When we say that we have '*thrown in the towel*', we mean that we have given up the fight. This is a **common** phrase.

In the following, choose the phrase that means nearly the same as the everyday expression.

1 **To bite the dust** means: (*a*) to fall and swallow a mouthful of dust; (*b*) to be defeated, or killed; (*c*) to test soil.
2 **To turn the tables** means: (*a*) to move the furniture around; (*b*) to learn one's tables at arithmetic; (*c*) to overcome one's enemies, after losing for a while.
3 **To send to Coventry** means: (*a*) to refuse to have anything to do with a certain person; (*b*) to act a play about Lady Godiva; (*c*) to buy a car from Coventry.

TEST 23

(A) Read through the following passage very carefully, and then answer the questions.

The Boastful Miller

By the side of a wood, in a distant country, ran a fine stream of water, and upon this stream there stood a mill. The miller's house was close by, and the miller had a very beautiful daughter. The miller was so proud of her that one day he told the king of the land, who used to come and hunt in the wood, that his daughter could spin gold out of straw.

Now, this king was very fond of money, and when he heard the miller's boast, his greediness was aroused and he sent for the girl to be brought before him. Then he led her to a chamber in his palace where there was a great heap of straw. He gave her a spinning-wheel, and said, 'All this straw must be spun into gold before morning, if you love your life.'

1   How do we know that the country was very far away?
2   What did the miller claim his daughter could do?
3   Why was the king in the wood?
4   The king had one great fault. Was it: (*a*) he was cruel to his subjects; (*b*) he was too fond of money; (*c*) he loved eating and drinking?
5   What task did the king set the miller's daughter to do?
6   When was the task to be completed?
7   The man and his daughter lived: (*a*) in a mansion near the sea; (*b*) in a thatched cottage in a village; (*c*) in a house near the mill on the banks of a stream?
8   The miller's daughter was: (*a*) good to look at; (*b*) unpleasant and ugly; (*c*) not very attractive?
9   How did the father earn his living: (*a*) by selling firewood to the people who lived near by; (*b*) by guiding travellers through the woods; (*c*) by grinding corn into flour?
10   Write down the words or phrases in the story that mean: (*a*) 'If you wish to remain alive'; (*b*) room; (*c*) claim.

(B) Sound-words

Sound-words are missing from these sentences. Choose suitable words to fill the spaces.

1 The logs were _______ on the fire.
2 The kettle was _______.
3 Ann's shout _______ across the hills.
4 The shutters were _______ in the wind.

(C) Alphabetical order

Write the names of these heavenly bodies in alphabetical order:

Pluto	Venus	Mars	Uranus
Neptune	Saturn	Jupiter	Mercury
	Earth	Asteroid	

(D) Nouns and adjectives

1 Here are four **nouns**: chair, witch, fox, mountain.

   And here are four **adjectives**: comfortable, cunning, snow-capped, ugly.

   Write the words together in suitable pairs.

2 Here are four other **adjectives**: humble, underground, flowery, well-filled.

   And here are the four **nouns**: stream, larder, peasant, border.

   Write the words together in suitable pairs.

(E) Homophones

Some words have a similar sound, but are spelt differently.

Example: *The **plane** flew into the sky. The army marched across the* ***plain***.

In the sentences below, choose the correct word from those inside the brackets:

1 The explorers rode their camels across the (**dessert, desert**).
2 The prisoner confessed his (**guilt, gilt**).
3 The fishmonger sells (**plaice, place**).
4 Have you a car for (**hire, higher**)?

TEST 24

(A) Read through the following passage very carefully, and then answer the questions.

On Treasure Island

Next morning the work of getting the treasure aboard began. I was kept busy packing the money into canvas bags. It took us three days, but at last the bars and coins were safely stowed away in the cabin.

We had seen nothing of the three pirates all this time, but we heard them singing and shouting as if they were drunk, or mad. A meeting was held, and it was decided that we must leave them on the island. We landed a good stock of powder and shot, tools, clothing, a sail, medicines, some rope, and a case of tobacco. Then we weighed anchor, and stood off the island. The three must have been watching us, for as we rounded the point we saw them kneeling on the sand with their arms raised, as if asking for mercy.

R. L. Stevenson

1 Read through these sentences, and then write down those that are true: (*a*) The treasure was being put into a cave. (*b*) It was being taken aboard ship. (*c*) It was being stowed away in a bank. (*d*) There were many jewelled swords and daggers. (*e*) There were many pearls and ornaments. (*f*) There were thousands of coins, and gold and silver bars.

2 How can we tell that there was a great deal of treasure?

3 At the meeting, what did they decide to do with the pirates?

4 What did they leave behind on the island: (*a*) for the pirates' health; (*b*) for hunting; (*c*) for smoking?

5 The ship 'weighed anchor'. Does this mean: (*a*) the sailors found the weight of the anchor; (*b*) they cut the anchor-rope, and let the ship drift; (*c*) the anchor was hauled up and taken aboard?

6 Why did the sailors think the pirates were asking for mercy?

7 The treasure was: (*a*) stored in bags made of canvas; (*b*) carried in leather wallets; (*c*) packed away in wooden cases?

Ⓑ Rhyming words

Now and **cow** are rhyming words. They have the same sound.

Write these twelve words in pairs, so that they rhyme:

tier	sage	thyme	new	role	gauge
flung	goal	pier	climb	flew	tongue

Ⓒ Synonyms

Look at the word **near**. Now look at the three words inside the brackets (close, distant, far). The word nearest in meaning to **near** is **close**, so we choose that.

Now do the same with these, choosing **one word** each time:

1 **purchase** (steal, buy, hide)
2 **valley** (glen, roadway, garden)
3 **ate** (refused, consumed, wasted)
4 **plump** (angry, fat, noisy)

Ⓓ Complete the poem

Choose, from the words in brackets, the most suitable word to finish the line of poetry:

Two little blackbirds singing in the (**hedge/morn/sun**)
One flew away and then there was one;
One little blackbird, very black and (**shy/tall/brave**)
He flew away and then there was the wall.
One little brick wall lonely in the (**field/garden/rain**)
Waiting for the blackbirds to come and sing again.

Ⓔ Choose the correct word

Look at the word FIRE. It need not be a **coal** fire or an **oil** fire, and it need not be **large** or **small**. But there must be **heat**.

Choose one word from those in the brackets that always has to do with the word before the bracket.

1 **husband** (house, wife, car)
2 **house** (fireplace, door, cellar)
3 **tree** (nest, roots, conkers)
4 **boot** (laces, sole, velcro)

TEST 25

A Read through the following verses very carefully, and then answer the questions.

Robin Hood

When Robin Hood was about twenty years old,
He happened to meet Little John,
A jolly, brisk blade, right for the trade,
For he was a lusty young man.

Though he was called Little, his limbs they were large,
And his stature was seven foot high;
Whenever he came, they quaked at his name,
For soon he would make them fly.

How they 'came acquainted I'll tell you in brief,
If you will but listen awhile.

1 At that time Robin was: (*a*) a boy; (*b*) an elderly man; (*c*) a young man; (*d*) a very old man?

2 What words tell us that Robin did not go on purpose to meet Little John?

3 'A jolly, brisk blade'. Does this mean: (*a*) a useful young man; (*b*) a very sharp knife; (*c*) a trusty sword; (*d*) a pretty piece of grass?

4 How can we tell that 'Little' was not a true description of Little John?

5 People 'quaked at his name'. Does this mean: (*a*) laughed out loud; (*b*) they shivered with fright; (*c*) they had never heard of him?

6 'Right for the trade'. Does this mean for: (*a*) selling fruit and vegetables; (*b*) driving a stage-coach; (*c*) fighting and duelling; (*d*) cutting wood?

7 'I'll tell you in brief.' What does 'in brief' mean?

8 'How they 'came acquainted.' Does this mean: (*a*) how they danced and sang; (*b*) how they met one another; (*c*) where they were born?

Ⓑ Put in order

The words in each of the following are in the wrong order. Rearrange them to make sentences.

1 Ball the window broke whose?
2 The sweet ate last Jack.
3 The gold perhaps will show the miser us.
4 A grate the fire in burned.

Ⓒ Crossword puzzles

Each of the answers to the following clues begins with the letters MON. Write down the words.

1 We buy things with it.   MON _ _
2 A king or queen.   MON _ _ _ _
3 Where monks live.   MON _ _ _ _ _ _
4 To watch over something.   MON _ _ _ _

Ⓓ Homonyms

The word **file** has more than one meaning. It may mean 'a tool for smoothing or cutting metal'; it may mean 'a line of soldiers'; or it may mean 'a container for papers'.

Write down the words that fit in with the following descriptions.

1 Part of a tree; part of an elephant; a piece of luggage.
2 A candle; an object that does not weigh very much.
3 Part of a ship; strict or rather fierce.
4 We might use this to light a fire; a game between teams.

Ⓔ Synonyms

The words in the first brackets mean something similar.

Choose a word of similar meaning from those in the second brackets.

Example: (*first, foremost, head*) – (*final, **leading**, prettiest*)

1 (vanish, perish, disappear) – (last, fade, continue)
2 (stake, post, pillar) – (trench, ditch, column)
3 (lead, start, begin) – (commence, end, destroy)
4 (fraction, piece, part) – (total, portion, addition)

TEST 26

(A) Read through the following passage very carefully, and then answer the questions.

Games

The children played many games in the busy roadway and on the pavement of the street in which they lived. A favourite game was Hopscotch, but this meant that untidy chalk marks were left behind, and there they stayed until the rain came and washed them out. Sometimes the children played noisier games such as 'Chase', or 'Tag', in which there was a great deal of running and shouting, and some danger.

The younger children sat in their own doorways playing with toys. There were always cars, building bricks, action figures and dolls, which the children shared between them.

Sometimes the older children played football or cricket. Everyone would join in the game called 'Statues', in which they had to stand as still as possible in a strange position, pretending to be carved from stone.

1 How can you tell that these children lived in a town, and not in the country?
2 Why was hopscotch an untidy game?
3 What, finally, got rid of the chalking?
4 Why were 'Chase' and 'Tag' noisy and dangerous games?
5 Why were doorways suitable places for playing with dolls: (*a*) because they were the doorways of dolls' houses; (*b*) because they were just off the busy pavements; (*c*) because no one lived in the houses?
6 How could you tell when the children were playing 'Statues'?
7 Choose a suitable title from these: (*a*) Grown-ups' Behaviour (*b*) Children's Fun (*c*) Animals' Antics.

B   **A or an?**

We speak of **a** girl and **a** street, but **an** egg and **an** iron. Write **a** or **an** in the spaces in the following sentences.

1   He put _______ iris and _______ aster with _______ lily.
2   She bought _______ book, _______ pen and _______ atlas.
3   _______ wren is smaller than _______ owl or _______ albatross.
4   The juice of _______ orange makes _______ good drink.

C   **Proverbs**

Complete these proverbs or well-known sayings:

1   A bad workman _______ _______ _______.
2   First come, _______ _______.
3   Look before _______ _______.
4   Let sleeping dogs _______.

D   **Choose the correct word**

From the words inside the brackets in each sentence, write down the one word that is nearest in meaning to the word in front of the sentence.

Example: ***difficult***. *The sum is (easy, **hard**, simple).*

1   **hastened**   They (strolled, hurried, walked) to school.
2   **wicked**   The man behaved in an (odd, evil, innocent) way.
3   **healthy**   That plant looks quite (fragile, hardy, weak).
4   **news**   What (pictures, drawings, information) have you?

E   **Capital letters**

Rewrite this paragraph, beginning each **proper noun** with a capital letter.

There was great excitement in the town when the queen of england visited. John brown arranged a concert at the majestic theatre, and her highness presented certificates to pupils of fairview primary school for good work in national savings. The orchestra played morning by grieg, and the town festival choir sang handel's messiah.

TEST 27

(A) Read through the following passage very carefully, and then answer the questions.

The Changeling Child

A mother once had her child stolen from her by the elves. Instead, they placed in the cradle a creature with a large head and staring eyes that would do nothing but eat and drink. So the mother went to one of her neighbours and asked her advice. The neighbour told her to carry the changeling into the kitchen and seat it on the hearth, then to light a fire and boil some water in two eggshells. This would make the changeling laugh, and it would be all over with him. The mother obeyed.

As she put the eggshells with the water in them on the fire, the little gnome-child began to laugh. At once a company of elves came crowding into the kitchen, bringing with them the woman's own child. Then they took up the changeling and disappeared with him.

1 Who stole the baby from the mother?
2 From where did they steal it?
3 How did the mother know that it was not her baby that was left?
4 The mother went: (*a*) to her own father and mother; (*b*) to someone living near by; (*c*) to the king of the country?
5 The creature was called a changeling because: (*a*) it often changed its shape; (*b*) it got out of the cradle and ran about the room; (*c*) the elves had exchanged it for a real baby?
6 What four things was the mother told to do?
7 Why did she do these things?
8 Which of these came into the kitchen: (*a*) a number of pixies; (*b*) a crowd of men and women; (*c*) a band of robbers?
9 What were they carrying with them?
10 What finally happened to the visitors and the changeling?

B **Word groups**

Australia, Brazil, China and Spain are all **countries**. Write down a general name for each of these groups.

1   goose, turkey, chicken, duck
2   grocer, butcher, greengrocer, fishmonger
3   tyrannosaurus rex, brontosaurus, pterodactyl, stegosaurus
4   strawberry, raspberry, loganberry, gooseberry

C **Anagrams**

In each case, rearrange the letters to make the name of an article of food.

Example: *GURAS becomes SUGAR.*

1   TEAM   3   TUTBER
2   DRABE   4   OCOAC

D **Rhyming words**

Write down this passage as it should be written, in verse. Begin each line with a **capital letter**.

And we will sit upon the rocks, and see the shepherds feed their flocks, by sunny rivers to whose falls, melodious birds sing madrigals.

E **Word ladders**

Beginning with the word BAD, and changing only one letter at a time, we can make the word COT.

Example: *BAD, CAD, CAT, COT.*

In the same way, change the word PAGE into the word BOOK.

PAGE

1   Anger.   _ _ _ _
2   An event at the sports. _ _ _ _
3   A framework of bars.   _ _ _ _
4   Found in and on earth.   _ _ _ _
5   A black bird.   _ _ _ _

BOOK

TEST 28

Ⓐ Read through the following passage very carefully, and then answer the questions.

The Island

When I was stranded on a desert island, I needed to make sure I was safe before I could think about escaping. The safest place to be was up in the trees, above the ground and the wild animals below. Ferocious meat-eating beasts were enticed towards me by the thought of having me for dinner.

I needed to build series of traps to help me. The ideal trap for a lion or a tiger is an iron cage and a bait of freshly-killed meat. Sadly, stranded alone as I was, I did not have any of this material. Crocodiles were also very difficult to handle, and I was careful to stay away from the water. Large snakes are more easy to deal with after they have had a good meal. Then they behave like human-beings who have over-eaten, I suppose. Smaller, more deadly snakes can be trapped by slipping bags over their heads. Catching birds or butterflies would be more to my liking!

1 What has to happen before the hero can think about escaping?
2 Where was the safest place to be?
3 Why was this place safe?
4 What makes the best trap for a lion?
5 Why did the hero not build these traps?
6 Why would a crocodile be difficult to handle: (*a*) because it lives in a foreign land; (*b*) because it cannot understand English; (*c*) because it has sharp teeth and a powerful tail?
7 When is the best time to catch a large snake?
8 Is this because: (*a*) It crawls happily into the trap. (*b*) It then becomes sleepy. (*c*) It wishes to rush about?
9 Why should a deadly snake have a bag slipped over its head: (*a*) because it likes to wear bags; (*b*) because it cannot see in the dark; (*c*) because it would not be able to use its deadly fangs?

10 Why would the writer be happier catching birds or butterflies?

B **Anagrams**

In each case, rearrange the letters to make the name of an animal.

1 O I L N   **3** O C O D I L E C R

2 B E Z R A   **4** N E T A H P L E

C **Choose the correct word**

A **splinter** is **a very small piece of wood**. Here are some other small amounts:

    ear   posy   lock   moment

Choose the correct ones to use with the following words:

    flowers   corn   time   hair

D **Joining words**

Below are pairs of sentences. Join each pair by using one of the following words: **which**, **whom**, **who**, **whose**. You may have to rearrange the words in some cases.

1 The guard blew the whistle. He is quite old.

2 I found the cricketer. Her score was the highest.

3 Here is the car. It was stolen.

4 Look at the girl. You scolded her.

E **Word endings**

Complete the words below by adding **ary** or **ery**, whichever is correct:

1 He taught in a **prim** _ _ _ school.

2 Mary went to a **second** _ _ _ school.

3 The **scen** _ _ _ was magnificent.

4 Modern **machin** _ _ _ was put into the factory.

TEST 29

(A) Read through the following passage very carefully, and then answer the questions.

The Circus

The circus had come to town. Through the High Street the happy procession made its way to the common, led by the band in their colourful uniforms. The trumpets and trombones gleamed in the sun, and the noise of the drum could be heard many streets away.

Koko, the chief clown, came next, with cartwheels and hand-springs to please everyone. His face was painted white, but his mouth was scarlet. His pointed hat always stayed on his head, although he seemed to spend most of his time upside-down. A string of elephants lumbered along, trunk to tail. Each had on its back a rider dressed in a silken jacket, and decorated with jewels. Of course, the gems were only imitation ones, but they looked real.

1   Where was the circus going to pitch?
2   Through what street did it have to pass?
3   Who were at the head of the procession?
4   How do we know that the band was playing loudly?
5   What two things could Koko do well?
6   How was Koko's face different from most people's faces?
7   Why was it surprising that Koko's hat stayed on his head?
8   Why does the story say 'a string' of elephants?
9   Why were the jewels imitations: (*a*) because real ones would have been too big; (*b*) because real ones would have cost too much; (*c*) because elephants do not like real ones?

(B) **Past tense**

Below is a story. The words in heavy type show that it is taking place **now**. Change these words so that the story happened in the **past**.

Today the sun **shines** brightly, and the birds **sing**. I **go** to the lake-side and **dive** into the clear water, where the rowing boats **glide** smoothly. Tom and I **paddle** across to the place where the train **begins** its journey. The guard **waves** to us.

C **Apostrophes**

Look at this sentence: Where is Bettys ball? The **apostrophe** is missing.

The sentence should have been: Where is Betty's ball?

Write out these sentences, putting the apostrophe in its correct place:

1 Jacks desk is broken.
2 The foxs cub is loose.
3 The foxes cubs are loose.
4 Johns dog is a spaniel.
5 Pams brooch is better than Marys.

D **Speech**

Look at these two sentences:

(a) *The girl said: 'I am eleven.'*
(b) *The girl said that she was eleven.*

In the first sentence the girl **speaks the words**. In the second sentence she does not actually speak. Change the following sentences so that the people are **actually speaking**.

1 The mate said that the boat was sinking.
2 She asked the way to the football ground.
3 The duchess told the servant to clear the table.
4 The pirate ordered him to walk the plank.

E **Word-doubles**

When we hear the word **knife** we often think of the word **fork**.

Write down the words that go with the following:

1 North and ______   4 Tooth and ______
2 Black and ______   5 Table and ______
3 Snakes and ______

TEST 30

(A) Read through the following phrases very carefully, and then answer the questions.

Fairy Song

Come follow, follow me,
You fairy elves that be,
Which circle on the green;
Come follow me, your queen.
Hand in hand, let's dance a round,
For this place is fairy ground.

When mortals are at rest,
And snorting in their nest,
Unheard and unespied,
Through keyholes we do glide;
Over tables, over stools, and shelves,
We trip it with our fairy elves.

1   Who is singing the song: (*a*) a mortal; (*b*) a giant;
(*c*) a goblin; (*d*) a fairy; (*e*) an ogre?
2   When is the dancing going to take place?
3   When mortals are 'snorting in their nest'. Does this mean:
(*a*) they are quarrelling; (*b*) they are reading; (*c*) they
are snoring; (*d*) they are sleeping peacefully?
4   How would the elves enter the rooms of the mortals?
5   'Circle on the green'. Does this mean: (*a*) ride cycles that
are green in colour; (*b*) dance in a circle on the grass; (*c*) play
with hoops, whilst wearing green clothes?
6   What does the word 'nest' mean in the poem?
7   What words or phrases in the poem mean: (*a*) unseen;
(*b*) move very silently?
8   'We trip it'. What does the phrase mean: (*a*) go on a trip, or
holiday; (*b*) stumble over the furniture; (*c*) dance lightly?
9   What is the difference between: (*a*) Let's dance a round.
(*b*) Let's dance around?

B **Who are these characters?**

What are the names of these people or creatures whom we read of in famous books?

1 He discovered the treasure chamber of the Forty Thieves.
2 She had three sisters: Meg, Beth and Amy.
3 They were all members of the Swiss Family ______.
4 He drank a potion that turned him into a monster.

C **Where do they live?**

A snail's home is its **shell**. What are the homes of these creatures?

1 spider   4 dog
2 bird   5 bee
3 wild rabbit   6 sheep

D **Complete the story**

Rewrite the paragraph below, using a word from the list to fill each of the spaces.

hollow	inn	tree	home
sleep	feathers	carrying	gold

He set to work to cut down the ______. When it fell he found, in a ______ under the roots, a goose with ______ of pure ______. He took it up and, ______ it under his arm, he went to a little ______ by the roadside. Here he decided to ______ for the night on his way ______.

E **Odd one out**

In each of the following groups of words, one word is out of place because it has nothing to do with the others.

Example: *goat, horse, **lion**, sheep, cow.*

Lion is the odd one out, because it is the only wild animal of the five.

Find the odd one out in these:

1 potatoes, wheat, oats, rye
2 army, brigade, fleet, regiment
3 knight, soldier, queen, pawn
4 rope, twine, glue, string